guide to
RUNNING

**the
physician
and
sportsmedicine**

guide to
RUNNING

ALLAN J. RYAN, M.D.

SERIES EDITOR, PAUL SCHULTZ

McGRAW-HILL BOOK COMPANY

NEW YORK   ST. LOUIS   SAN FRANCISCO   DÜSSELDORF
LONDON   MEXICO   SYDNEY   TORONTO

1 2 3 4 5 6 7 8 9 0   M U M U   8 7 6 5 4 3 2 1 0

LIBRARY OF CONGRESS CATALOGING IN PUBLICATION DATA
Ryan, Allan J
  The physician and sportsmedicine guide to running.
  Includes index.
  1. Running—Physiological aspects.   2. Running—Accidents and injuries—Prevention.   3.   Sports medicine.
I.   Title.
RC1220.R8R9   617′.1027   80-10336
ISBN 0-07-054358-5

Illustrations by Elton Hoff

Book design by Marsha Picker

acknowledgments

THE WRITING of any book is seldom completely the work of one person. The contributions of Paul Schultz as general editor, Cynthia Schultz and Peggy Bittner as typists and Elton Hoff as artist to this book are gratefully acknowledged.

contents

1.
why run?

BEYOND THE PREHISTORIC MISTS that obscure the circumstances of our development as human beings, one imagines that our anthropoid ancestors and their descendants were runners. Certainly the limited anthropologic evidence suggests that this was so. Human beings must have run to survive—both as hunter and as hunted. The fact that man could run probably has a great deal to do with our being here today, since it seems early homo sapiens had little brain power and few tools to aid his precarious existence. Later, of course, the runner served as a means of communication, and, as civilizations evolved, running was a primary activity in games and formal athletic competitions.

Running, it would appear, is absolutely basic to the nature and evolution of our species.

Today, we no longer run to get our fresh meat, and relatively few of us are or were competitive athletes. Yet some 24 million of us are running regularly and intensely, from jogging (slow running) to competing in grueling long distance events such as the Boston Marathon, which in 1979 had 12,000 entrants. From one point of view, this rage for running (and other forms of exercise) seems to be another aspect of "survival," that is, survival as healthy, well-functioning individuals who may—and this has yet to be proved—live longer because of it. While the effects of exercise in prolonging life or preventing cardiovascular and other degenerative diseases cannot be documented yet, biomedical investigators have shown that regular physical activity does produce a number of positive effects, among them improved blood capacity and pumping action of the heart; enhanced gas exchange in the lungs and more efficient delivery of oxygen to the tissues and organs; a decrease in the percentage of body fat; and a greater capacity of the body to work without excessive fatigue. (These and other effects will be discussed in greater detail later on.)

Moreover, persons who are well conditioned, especially those who have progressed from a sedentary life style to a regular exercise program, report a marked enhancement of virtually all functional aspects of their lives, emotional as well as physical.

In short, medical authorities can say that regular, vigorous exercise will improve your health. And I think everyone would agree that a healthy life is better than an unhealthy one, as relative as those terms may be for any given individual.

Which brings us in a rather roundabout way to your personal reasons for taking up running. Why do you want to run, and what do you expect to gain from it? These are reasonable questions to ask at the outset, because running, as fashionable as it may be nowadays, is at bottom hard work, especially for the beginner. It may be physically beneficial, personally satisfying, and at times exhilarating, but it is work, as you will discover if you launch a serious running program.

Nevertheless, if pursued regularly and sensibly, with proper warm-up and cool-down and other precautions, running will produce the benefits claimed for it. It will reduce body fat, increase endurance, tone the muscles, enhance the function of the body's systems, and probably improve your attitudes toward life in general.

But even beyond these personal benefits, the extraordinary popularity of running is probably due to its highly practical virtues: It can be done anytime, virtually anywhere, alone or with others. It is inexpensive; except for good-quality, well-fitted shoes, running requires no special clothing, uniform, or equipment. It needs no court, field, gym, or pool, nor the fees associated with a "place" to play. Most important, it requires no special aptitude or skill. Barring serious disease or physical handicap, anyone can run.

2.
what
happens
when
you run?

ALL BODILY MOVEMENT requires the expenditure of energy. In each individual, energy is available to meet the requirements of daily living activities and is expressed in terms of strength, endurance, speed, flexibility, balance, or other qualities of performance as required. Unless a person increases his or her activity considerably, these qualities are not improved but remain at a basal level.

Body systems respond to increased demands by improving their capacities to meet them. For this to happen, these systems must be overloaded systematically and progressively. The effects produced are known as effects of training. When a person who has not previously undertaken exercise more vigorous than walking starts running, then training effects begin to appear.

Running is more than just fast walking, in which the body weight is always supported on one foot or the other. Running is a series of jumps—the whole body is lifted free of the ground on each jump. In fact, the effective force on each landing foot is equivalent to about 2½ times the runner's body weight.

The major training effects of running are seen in the heart, lungs, muscles, and body fat. These effects are produced gradually, depending on the frequency and intensity of running, and are reversible when running stops completely.

Effects on the Heart

The heart is a muscle, and it responds to training as any other muscle does, by becoming thicker and stronger. Because it has to beat continuously (while other muscles contract only when called upon) and its contractions are controlled by a different nervous system, called the involuntary system, heart muscle has certain differences from skeletal muscle in structure and function. Consequently it is subject to other influences, particularly a person's state of mind and the capacity to respond to certain drugs that can stimulate, strengthen, or depress heart action. But the main concern here is how the heart is affected by regular, vigorous exercise, especially running.

When a person starts to run regularly, the heart muscle becomes thicker and stronger as the result of an increase in thickness of the individual muscle fibers. Since muscle is composed chiefly of proteins, and since the conversion into muscle of the proteins we take into our body for both growth and replacement is under the influence of hormones, notably the male hormone testosterone, the degree to which its growth will occur depends on the individual's age and sex. (Women have male hormones in their bodies, although in much smaller quantities than men do.) Heart muscle has a greater capacity for desirable growth in younger persons, but enlargement will occur to some extent even in older adults.

The heart muscle strengthened by exercise increases the force of its contractions so that it gives a more powerful push to the blood, and it contracts efficiently at a much higher rate than it does normally in a sedentary individual. If an untrained person becomes excited, the heart will beat very rapidly in response to emotional stress, but it will not be efficient in its contractions since it will pump out less blood with each stroke. The net result may be fainting, because less blood has been pumped to the brain. The heart that has been trained by exercise, however, compensates for its more rapid and forceful beating by dilating (enlarging) its chambers so it can accept and discharge more blood with each beat—to increase what we call its stroke volume.

The body further adapts to this situation by increasing the total amount of blood in circulation so that the heart's supply will be ample. This it does principally by increasing the liquid, or plasma, volume rather than the number of red blood cells.

This increase in heart size and volume can be observed if an X ray is taken from the front and the side of the heart with the individual in a standing position. It can also be detected less exactly by a physician examining the heart by ausculation and percussion, using his stethoscope and fingers, respectively. Some years ago when this phenomenon was noted, it was called "athlete's heart" and it was believed that the enlarged heart would shorten the athlete's life. Now we know that it is the sign of a strong and healthy heart, provided the heart does not have a disease that would weaken and distend the muscle and reduce its pumping efficiency.

Once this increase in heart size has been achieved by training, it can be maintained by exercising regularly three or more times a week. If exercise stops completely, however, the heart will decrease its stroke volume within a relatively short time, while the volume of blood in circulation also will return to baseline levels. The thickening of the heart muscle itself appears to persist because the heart continues to contract. Although we have no evidence of this from controlled studies (which might be impossible to obtain), indirect evidence suggests this thickening phenomenon continues. Moreover, persons who have trained their hearts when they were young seem to be capable of retraining themselves more rapidly than individuals who have never trained.

Effects on the Lungs and Respiration

Contrary to what one might expect, increasing the volume of the lungs is not the most important effect of exercise training. It is true that the ability to expand the lungs increases as a result of strengthening both the primary breathing muscles (the diaphragm and the muscles between the ribs, called the intercostals) and the secondary ones (the sternomastoids in front of the neck and the abdominals). More important, the ability to get more oxygen from the air through the respiratory system to the muscles is improved by an increase in what is called the perfusion rate in the lungs. This is accomplished chiefly by expanding the number of working capillaries that surround the air sacs, or alveoli.

Runners also learn to breathe more deeply and efficiently, regulating the timing of their breathing according to the length and frequency of their strides. This happens automatically for some, but has to be learned by others. Mouth breathing is essential to running since the volume of air required cannot be introduced through the nose alone.

In some persons, vigorous running for a period of five minutes or more may bring on a spasm of the breathing passages, or bronchi, which can be so severe that the person must stop running. This exercise-induced bronchospasm (EIB) can occur in persons who ordinarily experience no distress in breathing, as well as in the great majority of persons who have asthma. Some individuals are able to "run through" their breathing difficulty by temporarily slowing their pace. In most cases this problem can be circumvented, or at least reduced considerably, by taking a drug such as theophylline (a generic marketed under a variety of names), which will prevent bronchospasm, or by inhaling a substance called cromolyn sodium, which also prevents it by a mechanism that as yet is unexplained.

At the level of the muscle cell, the number and size of the mitochondria—the so-called powerhouse of the cells—are increased. This means a greater efficiency in the use of the oxygen that is transported by the red cells from the lungs to the muscles, since a greater percentage of it can be extracted by the muscle cells and more can be utilized per unit of time for the combustion of the carbohydrates, fat, and other energy-producing compounds in the cells.

Effects on the Muscles

Besides the heart and the muscles of respiration, many other muscles are used in running, but some are not over-loaded hard and often enough to produce a training effect. Strong action of the arms and shoulders as well as thighs and legs is important in running, yet running alone is not ordinarily sufficient to increase the strength or endurance of the muscles in the trunk and upper extremities. The runner must do special exercises to strengthen these muscles if their efficiency is to be improved.

Muscles in the hips, thighs, legs, and feet are strength-ened to some extent by the exercise of running, but strength does not continue to increase because the load that is sup-plied by the lifting of the body weight does not increase. In fact, if a person is overweight when he or she starts running, the load gradually decreases. When muscles are continually or repeatedly loaded with the same weight, they develop greater endurance, but this does not cause them to enlarge as they do when they increase in strength. The result is that a runner's muscles will remain relatively slender unless he or she is also doing special exercises to develop strength. This endurance capacity may last a relatively long time after running stops, but we don't know how long or to what ex-tent.

Muscle draws its energy from three different sources. For sprinting a short distance, the muscle uses creatine phosphate and adenosine triphosphate, as well as some of the glycogen that is stored in the muscle. It can derive energy from these sources without the air of oxygen through a process called anaerobic metabolism. As running continues for more than a minute or so, glucose is drawn from the blood into the muscle, converted to glycogen, and used as the main source of energy. The blood glucose in turn is replenished from glycogen that has been stored in the liver.

As running continues over a longer period, muscle uses fatty acids as its main source of energy. Some of the acids have been stored in the muscle, but the majority arrive via the blood from the various fat "depots" in the body. Although the body's carbohydrate reserves in the form of stored glycogen may be easily exhausted by a marathon run, stores of fat are sufficient to allow a person to carry on for three to four times that distance without replacement.

Changes in Body Composition

Because relatively large amounts of fat are consumed in the process of running distances of a few miles on a regular basis, runners will gradually reduce their weight by losing fat, until they reach a point of balance where intake equals consumption. Since some increase in muscle substance also occurs, there is a relative increase in lean body mass—the sum of the runner's muscle, bone, and organs. Body fat percentages decrease from what appear to be current norms of 20 to 25 percent for adult men and 25 to 30 percent for women to 15 to 20 percent and 20 to 25 percent, respectively, in those who run regularly. Competitive long distance runners may have as little as 5 to 8 percent body fat among men and 8 to 10 percent among women.

Thus, persons who run for recreation and exercise do not need to eat a special diet. They should have one that is well balanced, with carbohydrate, fat, and protein in proportions of roughly 70 percent, 20 percent, and 10 percent by weight, respectively. Many guides to such a balanced diet are available and a table covering basic foods appears later in this chapter. Moreover, a person who is healthy and well nourished does not require vitamin or protein supplements.

Competitive runners may find some advantage in increasing their carbohydrates and decreasing fats and proteins in the week before a race. The scheme of following an exhaustive run with a low carbohydrate diet for three days before loading up with carbohydrates for the next three days makes effective training too difficult for many people because they become too easily exhausted to maintain quality training during this period.

Most people prefer to take their daily running exercise in a fasting state in the morning or at least three hours after their last meal. Running soon after a meal is not harmful, although it may cause abdominal discomfort. It is better not to eat solid food closer than three hours to a race. Any food taken on the day of a race should consist chiefly of carbohydrates; however, drinking preparations containing carbohydrate in the form of sugar shortly before a race can cause a drop in blood sugar after the race begins, which can impair running efficiency.

Water is essential to runners. It should be taken freely before, during, and after running. The need for salts, specifically sodium and potassium, has been greatly overstated. Solutions containing more than small concentrations of salts and sugar may actually be detrimental to the runner

A Guide to Good Eating for Athletes*

Food groups	Foods	Number of servings daily†
Milk	Milk, cheese, ice cream, and other milk-based foods	4 or more glasses, or equivalent
Meat	Meats, fish, poultry, eggs, dry beans, peas, nuts	3 or more servings
Vegetables	Dark green, light green, yellow, potatoes	4 or more servings
Fruits	Citrus fruits, apples, juices, tomatoes	3 or more servings
Breads and cereals	Whole grain, enriched	4 or more servings

* The above will provide a well-balanced diet, adequate in all nutrients

† Servings in any category except fruits can be increased to add more calories

because absorption of water from the small intestine may be delayed. If too concentrated, such solutions may draw water out of the circulatory system into the intestines.

Effects on the Mind

When a sedentary person starts to exercise regularly, changes in thinking and attitude take place. Some of these changes occur as results of changes in the person's way of living to accommodate the demands of an exercise program. Others stem from the effects of the exercise itself. The former result from the voluntary desire and willingness to make the necessary changes. The latter take place for reasons we do not completely understand.

When a person alters his or her way of living, this influences to some extent the attitude toward not only personal life but relationships with family and friends, as well.

A person who starts a running program may find that the morning is the most convenient time to exercise. This means arising earlier so that running, showering, and dressing can be done before breakfast. For a person who has been accustomed to sleeping late, the quiet of the early morning could be a revelation—a change in attitudes not only toward the whole day but also toward the places where one lives and works.

If the evening proves to be the most convenient time for running, a different change may occur. Activities may have to be postponed, rearranged, or canceled. The other family members may have to adjust meal times and social activities, get used to sweaty running clothes, and be willing to get involved in a new topic of conversation. They may also have to adjust to a change in the runner's personality. If the runner becomes involved in competition, further dislocations occur, involving trips, absences from home, and often the necessity of providing support for the runner.

Although running in its most basic form ordinarily involves little expense, once a person becomes involved, shoes are purchased frequently, special clothing becomes appealing, and expenses for trips and entry fees have to be included in the budget. The runner may have to take time off from work or use vacation days for participation in competitive events. All of these create changes in attitudes and relationships.

One of the attractions of running as an exercise is the feeling of well-being (sometimes called "positive feedback") that ordinarily arises during running and may last up to several hours afterward. This exhilaration may spring from the increases in body temperature and metabolic rate that accompany running or perhaps from changes in hormone balance. The recently described brain substances called endorphins, which mediate or mitigate the brain's response to painful stimuli, seem to be related to feelings of pleasure, and their activity may be increased by vigorous exercise.

The so-called runner's high begins for most people after they have been running continuously for at least 30 minutes. Changes in appreciation of one's surroundings, including colors and other subjective judgments, sometimes resemble descriptions of experiences with certain mind-altering drugs. Emotional changes may be so profound that some persons are moved to tears, not because they are sad but because they are so intensely happy and in tune with their surroundings.

Because of its potential for inducing positive emotional change, running is being used in the treatment of persons suffering mental disturbances characterized principally by depression. Several psychiatrists have reported successful treatment of such patients by individual or group running sessions. Since interaction with the therapist in the course of treatment seems to be important, a number of therapists have become active runners as well.

3.
a
program
for
running

WHEN YOU START TO RUN, you usually have a very general objective in mind—to have a pleasant, beneficial experience. Once you get involved, you begin to think more about why you are running and what you wish to accomplish. The initial experience may be unpleasant, even painful. At this point, if you are not too discouraged to continue, it helps to define your immediate running objectives. If you want to reach and maintain a state of physical fitness, then the most important advice at the beginning is don't push too hard. Alternate walking with running at the start. You'll notice I don't use the term "jogging," although it is a popular one, because people use it to mean several

different things. Originally it meant a flat-footed shuffle at
a slow rate, barely different from walking. It has a very brief
float phase when both feet are off the ground. To the average runner today, it means a slow pace for cooling down
after a run. To the competitive runner it is running at a
pace slower than seven minutes a mile.

A sensible schedule to begin with is to alternate walking
100 yards and running 100 yards for half a mile. After a
week, this should be comfortable, and you can increase your
running distance to 150 to 200 yards, keeping the walking
distance the same and covering a mile. After 10 to 14 days
at this schedule, you should be able to run a mile without
walking. When this distance comes easily, add increments
of half a mile or so each week until you are running 3 to 4
miles. If physical fitness is your objective, 20 to 30 minutes
of continuous running is sufficient for this purpose. Let me
add, though, that 5 to 10 minutes for warming up and an
equal amount for cooling down are absolutely necessary.

The purpose of warming up is to increase body temperature by several degrees. At higher than normal temperatures, muscles become more plastic and less susceptible to
being torn by the sudden, forceful contractions characteristic of sports. This is particularly important on a cold day,
when muscles may be abnormally stiff. The increased temperature also shortens reflex times so that the body reacts
more quickly to all situations it encounters.

Working your upper and lower extremities through
their normal ranges of motion also helps to prevent injuries
to the ligaments that hold the joints together. However,
you should not overstretch your muscles immediately before
calling on them for maximal contractions, since this will

make them more susceptible to an injury. If you need heavy stretching of muscles, especially the hamstrings which have a tendency to shorten in runners, you should do this after running, not before.

A good series of warming-up exercises is illustrated in Figures 1 through 6 at the end of this chapter. You may have others that you prefer. Which ones you do is not really important as long as you do them energetically.

When you have finished running, it is better not to stop abruptly to sit or lie down. Instead, keep moving around slowly for 5 to 10 minutes until you have had a chance to cool down a bit and catch your breath. If you have been running hard, a slow jog for a quarter-mile or so would be appropriate. If you have stretching to do, this is also the best time, when the muscles are warm and pliant.

The reason for cooling down gradually is to help the muscles eliminate the accumulated lactic acid more quickly and to avoid the stiffness in the muscles that can result later on from an abrupt halt in exercise. If you have been running outdoors on a cold day with only light clothing, you should put on your warm-up suit before engaging in your cool-down activity, to avoid the effects of a sudden chill.

In the beginning you will find that you make more rapid progress and are more quickly rid of the early discomforts of running if you can run every day, or at least every other day. Once you have developed a desirable degree of fitness, you can maintain this state by running only three days a week or, for best results, every other day. Running only twice a week is not enough to retain training effects, while running every day increases the risk of an overuse injury.

If your objective is to become a competitive runner, a

slow start is still best. You will want to increase your daily mileage beyond 4, however, with the amount depending on the competitive distance you have selected. If you are not involved in interscholastic, intercollegiate, or club running on the track, the most popular distances for road races are 3 miles, 5,000 meters, 6 miles, 10,000 meters, and the marathon, which is 26 miles 385 yards. So-called mini-marathons at distances of 10 to 15 miles have also become popular recently.

When training for competition, some runners like to run every day, others 4 to 5 times a week. The total number of miles in a week may vary from 25 to more than 100, depending on the individual's preference, the event for which he or she is training, the season of the year, and other factors. In general, the heavier the training load, the greater the possibility of sustaining an injury from overuse. Runners who have been covering 25 to 30 miles a week and suddenly double their mileage to prepare for a long race also increase their risk of injury.

Competitive runners are interested in their speed as well as their endurance. Consequently, they will schedule some workouts at relatively short distances and concentrate on speed, while running others at long distances to cultivate a steady pace. Sometimes they will introduce a sprint in the middle or at the end of a run.

The intensity of a running workout is an important factor in developing and maintaining physical fitness, as well as in preparing for competition. Different styles of training are favored by different coaches and runners, and some of these have become identified by particular names, such as "long slow distance (LSD)," "speed play," "interval training," and "pace training."

Long slow distance running is usually carried out at a steady pace. The intensity of the workout, therefore, depends on how long you run and the pace that is maintained. The judgment of pace comes with experience; most runners can distinguish between paces that differ by as little as one minute per mile.

In speed play, the runner covers perhaps as much distance as in LSD, but will alternate slow pace with short bursts of speed running. The purpose is not only to provide variety to the run, but, by increasing the intensity periodically, to place a greater work load on the cardiorespiratory system and thus improve the runner's efficiency.

The system of interval training involves running relatively short distances at a rapid but steady pace with a very short period of rest and recovery after each fast run. This system is used more by competitive than recreational runners. A distance runner might run a series of quarter-miles in 1 minute, with only 1 minute's rest after each effort, or half miles in 2¼ minutes, with 2- to 3-minute rest intervals. Intensity can be increased by shortening the time to complete each run, reducing the rest interval, or both. The effect is to improve speed plus anaerobic capacity, the ability to run effectively with a substantially reduced oxygen supply.

Pace training is somewhat similar to interval training but the progression from a slower to a faster pace is planned progressively over a period of days or weeks, at or near the distance that is to be run in competition. It is often combined with interval work.

Runners do not restrict themselves exclusively to any one of these training methods but may use several or all at different times, depending on their needs. You may wish to experiment with them to introduce some variety into your program.

The Mechanics of Running

Running is a natural activity, yet good running form does not come naturally to most people—it has to be learned. Attention to a few basic habits of body position and running stride will make your running more efficient and safer.

In slow jogging, form is relatively unimportant, so long as it is comfortable. In running, however, form becomes important for establishing economy of motion and helping to prevent injury. In sprinting, form may make the difference between fair and good performance.

In contrast to walking, during which the body is always supported on one foot or the other, running is a series of small jumps, with a period of support and a period of flight when neither foot is in contact with the ground. Since the propulsive action of the body muscles can be exerted only when there is contact with the ground, it is obviously advantageous to keep the flight phase relatively short. The more times the feet hit the ground (stride rate) during any given run, the greater will be the propulsive force during that period. Yet running is also concerned with covering distance, so efficiency also relates to the distance covered in each stride (stride length). The runner must reach a compromise between the two, depending on his or her objectives.

A very rapid stride rate is effective in sprinting, since it increases the number of propulsive efforts per unit of time. Such rates can be maintained only for relatively short periods, however, because the energy cost soon outstrips the ability of the body to supply the necessary oxygen and fuel to the muscles. Stride length is shortened, yet it must not be too short to ensure efficiency and cover sufficient ground.

In running middle and long distances, the best runners have a stride length (measured from one foot contact to the next foot contact) of about 1.5 meters at a stride rate (total of right and left foot-ground contacts per minute) of about 190. A study of college runners showed that they tended to shorten their strides over a 4-year period as they improved their running times. One reason for this is that oxygen demand increases disproportionately as stride becomes longer. Studies of female runners show that they have shorter stride lengths than men (due to shorter leg lengths), but have longer relative stride lengths (ratio of leg length to stride).

Because running efficiency depends on progress in a horizontal direction, excess motion in the vertical plane tends to diminish this efficiency. Thus, excessive bouncing with each stride slows the runner, as does placing the legs or feet out to the sides or swinging the arms excessively across the body or out to the sides. Women runners demonstrate a greater vertical lift than men on the average. The best runners show very little vertical lift.

Cinematic analysis of running form shows that in good runners the leg is never fully extended on the knee, except in a sprint start where the body is angled sharply forward. During the swing phase of the thigh and full leg while in flight, the hip and knee are both flexed, with some runners bringing the heel almost up to the buttocks. Just before the foot hits the ground, the hip is extended slightly as knee flexion is reduced. As the foot takes off, the leg is still flexed about 10 degrees.

The pelvis rotates slightly as the thigh is brought up into flexion and then reverts as the foot makes contact with the ground. The movement of the opposite arm should be just sufficient to balance the pelvic rotation in the opposite direction.

A question that sometimes concerns runners unnecessarily is how much forward lean they should adopt. Except perhaps as two runners approach the finish line very close together, forward lean is not important. What is important is to keep your back as straight as possible. An excessive curvature, or sway, in the lower back is often a problem in runners who have overdeveloped their hamstring muscles in other sports and have lost flexibility in their hip joints. It prevents the necessary hip flexion in the swing phase, which in turn prevents achieving optimum stride length and weakens the propulsive force at takeoff.

Persons with an excessive sway, or lordosis, in their lower spine usually have not learned how to stand and walk properly, and carry their poor posture over to running. This fault can be corrected by learning how to rotate the pelvis forward by tightening the abdominal muscles and pulling down the buttocks muscles. You can practice this by standing with your back toward the wall, touching it with your shoulders and heels, and then trying to flatten your back against it.

If you are seriously interested in improving your running form, and consequently your efficiency, an analysis by an experienced running coach is a necessity. The coach will almost certainly want to make a videotape of your running form from both front and side views, then study it in slow motion. This may be a bit expensive, but it can be well worth it in terms of preventing injury as well as improving your competitive ability.

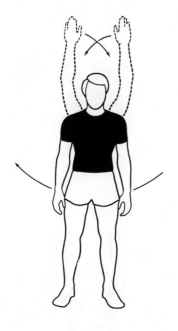

WARM-UP EXERCISES

figures 1-a and **1-b** Arm circling. Standing with your feet about 12 inches apart, raise your arms out to the side, up over your head and then swing them down across your body in front and return them to your sides. After 5 rotations in one direction, reverse the direction for 5 rotations and then repeat the whole cycle of 10 for a total of 20 rotations.

figures 2-a and **2-b** Lateral bending. In a standing position with feet about 12 inches apart raise both arms over your head. Bend your trunk as far as possible to your left, lowering that arm and hand to your side. Return to an upright position and then repeat to your right side. Do 5 repetitions to each side.

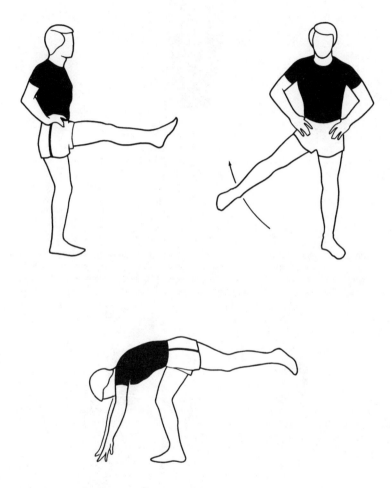

figures 3-a, 3-b, and **3-c** Leg raising. In a standing position with hands on your hips raise your right leg forward as far as you can; return to your starting position. Repeat with your left leg. Raise your right leg sideward, and return to your starting position. Repeat with your left leg. Raise your right leg to the rear, bending your trunk forward, and try to touch the floor with your hands. Return to your starting position and repeat with your left leg. Repeat each position 9 times.

figure 4 Side straddle hop. From a standing position with feet together jump up, extending each leg directly out to its own side and at the same time raise your arms from your sides bringing them up over your head. Return to your starting position. Repeat 9 times.

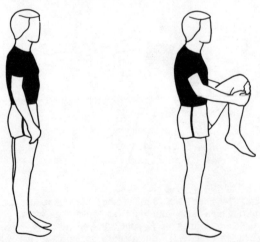

figures 5-a and **5-b** Knee raises. In a standing position with feet together, raise your left knee bringing it up to your chest with both hands. Return to your starting position and repeat with your right leg. Repeat the whole cycle 9 times.

figure 6 Calf stretcher. Place one foot ahead of the other about 2 feet in a stride position with the forward knee flexed and the rear leg extended. Lean forward until a stretch is felt in the rear calf. Hold for 10 seconds and repeat with the opposite leg. Repeat 4 times on each side.

4.
your
running
equipment

Clothing

WHEN YOU RUN, you want to wear clothing that is as lightweight as possible and that will not restrict the free movement of your arms or thighs. At one period in ancient Greece male athletes competed in games without clothing. We don't know the reason for this, but it may have been their way of combating heat stress by allowing free perspiration of the entire body. There is no evidence that girls and women were unclothed for their sport competition, but they may have been. It is doubtful that there is any advantage to running in the nude, with the exception of avoiding friction on the nipples in long distance races; in the case of women with sizable breasts, there is a definite advantage in having a good breast support. Certainly few runners today who are used to wearing shoes at other times would enjoy running shoeless, except possibly on a beach or a well-kept golf course.

The traditional running outfit is a singlet and shorts. Some men run in long-distance races in warm weather without the shirt, but this is not considered proper dress for most competitions on the track. Except when it is hot and humid, the runner should wear a warm-up suit over the basic outfit. The suit consists of a pullover or buttoned shirt or jacket with a low collar and long sleeves and a pair of long trousers, pullover style or zipped down the legs.

Since the T-shirt is the most popular all-purpose garment today, it is frequently worn by men and women in long-distance races.

Whether a man wears a supporter under his shorts is a matter of personal preference. It is apt to be a source of chafing in long distance races, and most running shorts worn today have a built-in panty. Women usually wear a bra unless their breasts are very small.

The Shirt. The best singlets today are constructed partly of nylon tricot, usually the top half or a band across the breasts, and a 50/50 blend of cotton and nylon tricot mesh. The armholes are cut wide to avoid binding and chafing, while the lower part is cut generously enough so that it does not pull out of the shorts too easily.

T-shirts are available in cotton and nylon tricot. The former are favored, chiefly because of the many pictures and inscriptions with which they can be emblazoned, and because they are more comfortable under warm-up suits in cold weather. Nylon shirts are made with a combination of mesh and solid material as are the singlets.

The Shorts. Although both cotton and nylon tricot are available in a variety of styles, the latter are more comfortable and popular, except in very cold weather. The better shorts have a built-in panty supporter, which in women's shorts has a cotton center panel. Some shorts are cut diagonally, with a wide opening for the legs to avoid binding. But a more popular feature today is the side slit, either as a V or with a flap over it so that the slit is hidden when not running.

The Warm-up Suit. These may be made of cotton-polyester blends, flannel, wool, or nylon tricot. Some of the tops are pullovers, some have partial zippers in front, some have full zippers, and some are fastened with snaps. Some contain pockets, others do not. The warm-up suit should be cut generously across the shoulders and around the upper arms. Some have elastic waistbands, some have drawstrings, and some have neither. Those made of nylon usually have neck panels across the shoulders for ventilation.

The trousers typically have an elastic waistband and a zipper along the side of each leg; some have elastic cuffs. Few have pockets.

Rain Gear. Windproof and waterproof nylon suits with neck panels across the shoulders, high collar, and hood (usually detachable) can be worn over shirts and shorts in warm weather and over a warm-up suit in cold, snowy weather. They are generously cut and usually close with zippers.

Cold-Weather Gear. Cotton shorts and a T-shirt under a wool warm-up suit are generally the most comfortable for running in cold weather. A nylon windbreaker may be worn over the top or a rain suit over all. If the warm-up suit doesn't have a hood, a wool cap that fits over the ears is essential. With any other type of headgear the runner should wear ear muffs. A pair of lined gloves or mittens is very important since very cold hands will lower the body temperature quite rapidly and expose the fingers to possible frostbite.

Wool socks help prevent frostbite of the toes, but cramming several pairs of socks in your running shoes may promote frostbite by cutting off the circulation. You may want to wear long socks to keep your legs warm as well. In very cold weather, men should wear extra protection for their genitals to avoid frostbite.

A face mask is desirable when the wind-chill factor is high. Wool is the best material, and the type that pulls over the head, with holes for the eyes, nose, and mouth, is the most comfortable.

The Socks. Many runners prefer to run without socks. If you are going to wear them, though, a light cotton or a cotton-synthetic blend will be the most comfortable, except in cold weather when wool or a wool-synthetic sock is better. It is important that the socks fit snugly, but not so tightly that they constrict the toes. Loose-fitting socks will slip down in your shoes and possibly cause blisters. The peds, which fit entirely inside the shoe, are a reasonable compromise.

Head Gear. Headbands of some absorbent material help to keep sweat out of the eyes and hold back the hair. Caps are popular with some runners as sunshades. They should have mesh tops to allow heat to escape from the head.

The Running Shoe

You can run in your bare feet, in combat boots, or in tennis shoes, but if you are running regularly and don't always have a choice of the surface on which you run, you should buy a pair of shoes made specifically for running. Only a few years ago you would have had a small choice of such footwear, but today there are dozens of styles and brands. No attempt will be made here to describe or list them all. Instead, I will outline the basic qualities that should be found in a good running shoe and the types that are best suited to different purposes.

The classic track shoe made of light glove leather with thin spikes on the sole and no heel is made only for sprinters. A similar shoe with a low rubber heel is still used by some middle-distance runners who compete only on a track. Recreational and long-distance runners need a sturdier shoe and have no need for spikes.

Shoes with the upper part made of leather will generally be more comfortable because they tend to adapt themselves to the shape of the foot, whereas nylon and other synthetics do not stretch and they cause the feet to perspire excessively. This is important since feet come in many shapes as well as sizes. Some shoes are made in only one width for each length, which is fine if you have a narrow foot, but such shoes can cause pressure problems for the broad-footed runner. Nowadays, however, good shoes are available in a range of widths.

The sole of the running shoe should be moderately flexible to allow the foot to bend slightly as it rolls from supination (the sole turned slightly up and in) through pronation (the transverse arch flattened toward the ground) and on to resupination as push-off occurs from the head of the first metatarsal (bones between the toes). If the sole is too flexible, it will allow too much pronation; if it is too stiff, not enough. It should be stiffened through the shank to prevent excessive pronation. The sole should also be well cushioned to absorb as much shock of impact as possible.

The inner sole should be lined, preferably with a material called Spenco that will respond to torque as well as uni-directional stress, to minimize the tendency to blistering. If it is not, such insoles can be purchased separately. Most running shoes today are built up toward the outer side of the foot to a point behind the metatarsal heads.

If the upper part of the shoe is constructed in such a way that the lacing comes down to the base of the toes, this may cause constriction. When you try on a shoe, you should be able to press the broad side of your thumb (outside the shoe) down to the inner sole between the tip of the shoe and your large toe. This will help to prevent blistering at the tips of the toes and hemorrhaging under the toenails. The toe box height from the insole, measured at 1 inch from the tip of the shoe, should be 1 inch.

The heel counter should be stiff, to keep the heel from rolling either in or out, and it should be lightly padded over the point of attachment of the Achilles tendon. In addition, the shoe should have a good padded cuff around its top. The depth of the heel from the insole to the top of the Achilles pad should be about 3 inches, and the inside of the heel should provide a well-cushioned cup.

When considering a pair of running shoes, it's a good idea to place them on a counter side by side with the heels pointing toward you. They should be symmetrical and not slanted toward or away from each other at different angles.

In some shoes sold today, the plantar surface of the heel is flared out to provide greater stability. This is not necessary for most runners and may create problems for some. In other shoes, the material of the sole is extended up onto the heel to retard wear at that point. The heel should be built up about 1 inch on a platform that rises gradually from about mid-foot.

The sole of the shoe may be smooth, may contain multiple small, very short cleats, or may be incised with a pattern of cuts and depressions to improve traction. There are running shoes available with ripple soles, but they are not popular with many runners because they impart a slight forward thrust and are somewhat heavier. Otherwise, the sole you select is chiefly a matter of personal preference since no one type has a particularly great advantage over another.

Training shoes are generally heavier than competition shoes because they are designed to take greater wear and absorb more shock. An additional advantage is that when the runner puts on competition shoes they feel very light on the feet. The sole of the competition shoe will usually be more flexible than that of the training shoe.

A good running shoe should cost between $25 and $40, although some may cost more. Shoes costing less are probably of poor quality—they won't stand up to long wear and they lack the desired protective qualities. To lengthen shoe life, wear them only for running and dry them slowly (away from heat) if they become wet.

An orthotic is any type of pad or removable support placed in a shoe to relieve stress in any part of the foot by correcting distribution of body weight through the foot. These vary from a simple metatarsal bar or wedge (sometimes called a "cookie" when used under the longitudinal metatarsal arch) made of felt, plastic, or foam rubber through a soft readymade support for the whole or part of the foot to a soft or rigid plastic support made from a plaster cast of the foot. If you need a special support because of a foot problem, you should consult an orthopedist or a podiatrist for advice on exactly what you need. Attempting to do it yourself may make matters worse.

If you have been given an orthotic to wear in your running shoe, remember that most of the shoes sold today already have some sort of built-in correction. This should be removed from the shoe (it will usually be necessary to remove the insole first) before placing your custom-made orthotic in the shoe.

5.
your
running
environment

Where Will You Run?

YOU MAY BE lucky enough to live where you can run regularly the year 'round in reasonable comfort and safety—at a high school or college track, a "Y" gymnasium, a golf course, a park, or on a path through the woods or simply some nice country roads. Even in such relatively secure and convenient environments you may have problems that are common to runners everywhere. Then, too, if you are serious about competitive running, you may travel to places where you may face unfamiliar problems; or, if you are adventurous and like some change from the familiar sights and sounds, you may find yourself in even more distant and remote locations.

Some of the things you will have to think about in both familiar and unfamiliar environments are the surfaces on which you run; the other traffic that passes over these surfaces, whether human, animal, or vehicular; the availability of toilet facilities; and even the social and political customs of the local inhabitants. Remarkably, there are relatively few places in the world where you can't run if you are properly prepared.

The greatest long-distance runner of whom we have any records was the Norwegian Mensen Ernst. In 1830, at the age of 29, after a 9-year period during which he gave running exhibitions in all major cities of Europe, he ran from Alexandria, Egypt, to Jerusalem in 6 days, most of it through trackless desert country, fording or swimming rivers where there were no bridges. In 1832, he ran the 1,600 miles between Paris and Moscow in 13½ days. And after resting a few days, he ran back. Finally, in 1836 he ran from Constantinople (Istanbul) to Calcutta, a distance of more than 4,000 miles in 30 days, running through deserts and over high mountains, and swimming rivers when necessary.

Ernst knew nothing of the information that science has made available to us today about the problems he faced, but he must have been very diplomatic to deal with the many different peoples he encountered—including bandits who held him up twice along the way—and very alert to the wild animals that abounded along his routes. His chief support came from a superbly conditioned body and a supreme self-confidence. You, on the other hand, can call on a substantial body of knowledge and a superior technology to help you on your way, wherever it may lead you. In this section, we will examine the problems and potential solutions related to your running environment.

People

The sight of a person running in some type of recreational clothing no longer excites the interest in this country and in many foreign countries that it once did. It may evoke some comments from sidewalk bystanders or groups of children. Some of the remarks are rude or sarcastic, but most are benign or even encouraging. Unless you are running at night (and are not wearing a fluorescent strip diagonally across your chest) or in a residential area, you will not ordinarily attract the attention of cruising police, as long as you don't cross a street illegally or run through a red light.

Be careful not to run across private property, unless you have specific permission to do so. Streets and roads through privately owned real estate developments are often restricted and not always posted at all points of access. Public roads, especially in parks, may be closed at certain times and trespassers subject to arrest.

The natives are not always friendly. Even though you may not be carrying anything of value, except perhaps a wristwatch, you may be assaulted and robbed of that or your running shoes. Female runners have been attacked sexually and even killed. You may be viewed as unfriendly by the locals because of your color, your different speech, or because you are a foreigner. Although there is no absolute safety in numbers, you will be much better off if you run with others when in a strange or possibly hostile environment. Also, a loud whistle carried on a cord around your neck is a useful protective device. It may startle a potential attacker, even if it doesn't succeed in summoning help.

Running alone in the dark hours, whether in the city or the country, is especially dangerous, not only because streets and highways are usually less traveled, but because many persons you will encounter may have had their suspicions, prejudices, or inclinations to violence fortified by liquor.

Animals: Mammals, Birds, Reptiles, Insects

The dog is frequently a danger to a runner, whether the animal is friendly or unfriendly. The friendly dog may jump at or on the runner by way of greeting or trip him by running in front of or between his legs. The unfriendly dog usually is defending his territory, may have an active dislike for people he doesn't know, and may become unduly excited by the sight of persons running (as the dog sees it) either at him or away from him. Neither type is apt to be dissuaded from his attention to you by soft ("nice doggie"), peremptory ("go home"), or angry ("stop, dammit") words.

A stick is very effective in protecting yourself from loose dogs. Unless trained for police work or to protect someone's property, dogs will shy away from a stick. If they are reluctant to recognize the stick's authority, a sharp rap will usually remind a dog of it and send him another way. Cans of sprays offensive to dogs are awkward to carry, apt to run out of substance at a critical moment, and generally are not very effective.

Wild animals may be encountered in some remote areas. Generally speaking, they are anxious to avoid human contact and will go out of their way to do so. Mothers with their young will attack, however, if they feel threatened, and bears are particularly unpredictable in their behavior. Your best tactic in encountering a wild animal on a run is to stop and give it a chance to look you over and move on. If he is inclined to stay in your path, either take a wide swing around him or go back the way you came. Usually you will not be able to outrun an attacking animal. You are better off trying to frighten him off by yelling or swinging a stick if you have one handy. Otherwise, try to get to a place where the animal can't go.

Geese and swans, frequently found in parks and around water holes on golf courses, are notoriously bad-tempered and will attack without warning. Give these birds a wide berth if you want to avoid a painful bite.

Smaller flying birds have been known to attack the heads of runners for reasons no one but the birds know. Ostriches are also short-tempered, but would rather run than fight. Unless you run in zoos, the problem may never come up.

Snakes will escape from humans if given a chance. Your greatest chance of being bitten, unless you are foolishly trying to handle one, comes from stepping on a snake accidentally. Rattlesnakes and water moccasins will attack if they feel threatened on home territory, so avoid running in areas these species are known to frequent. If you are bitten, don't attempt to treat yourself unless you are in a remote area. Get medical attention as quickly as possible, but don't run for it. Running speeds the flow of venom in the bloodstream.

Flies and mosquitoes can be annoying, particularly

when you encounter a swarm. If it is the appropriate season
and you know you are in an area where you are likely to
encounter them, use an insect repellent spray on your exposed skin before you run. Wasps, hornets, and bees usually will not attack unless you get into a swarm or step on a
nest. If you know that you are allergic to insect venom, you
should carry an insect-sting kit during bug season. Anaphylactic shock can be averted by a prompt injection of epi-
nephrine. If you are running in a country where malaria is
endemic, you should protect yourself by the prophylactic
use of an antimalarial drug.

Vehicles

Cars, motorcycles, and bicycles all pose hazards to the
runner. You can avoid a good deal of trouble by learning
their rules of the road, as well as the regulations that apply
to pedestrians. You are expected to obey traffic signals
wherever you are.

Regulations concerning running vary from place to
place, but generally it is safest to run facing vehicular traffic.
Remember, though, that if you do this consistently on a
road with a crown, you will be off balance. This can lead to
a knee problem on the leg that is lower or to back strain. If
you have a choice, run with and against traffic on alternate
days.

If you are going to be running at night, dusk, or dawn,
you should have fluorescent markers on your clothing, a
wrist band with a flashlight, or some other device that
makes you more visible to vehicle drivers.

When running in a strange city or other area, it is a
good idea to carry a map. If there are no outstanding land-

marks to guide you, a compass is very useful too. When running in a foreign country, a basic phrase book can be invaluable if you get lost and don't speak the language.

Bicycle paths are open to runners in some areas but not in others. If the regulations aren't posted, be sure to ask before using such a path. If you do run on a bike path, always keep to the right and be alert for the sound of a bell or a whistle behind you.

Surfaces

Streets and roads may be dirt, gravel, macadam, or concrete. City sidewalks are usually concrete, but they also exhibit the same variety. Bicycle paths ordinarily are macadam, while running trails may be dirt or wood chips. Tracks are often made of compacted cinders, but they may vary in composition from brick dust to a synthetic such as Tartan. Board tracks may be encountered outdoors as well as indoors. Many multipurpose indoor facilities now have floors completely covered with artificial turf. Athletic fields of grass and golf courses are available to runners in some areas.

With properly cushioned running shoes, it should be possible to run comfortably on any surface. People may be individually susceptible to stress injuries on harder surfaces, depending on previous running experience, level of conditioning, age, and other variables. Surfaces such as dirt and grass vary greatly in their relative hardness according to the climate and the amount of traffic over them. Sand may be very loose or very hard packed, and running over it in bare feet may provoke problems of leg pain and foot sprains for those used to running in shoes on other surfaces.

Running regularly on concrete or on a plastic surface laid directly over concrete probably produces a higher percentage of stress fractures than running on any other surface.

Artificial turf surfaces vary a great deal in their relative hardness according to the type of cushioning and base on which they are laid. This is dictated by what is expected to be the predominant use of the surface. A field used principally for baseball will have a much firmer support than one used chiefly for football. As the turf ages, the pile tends to mat down, decreasing its ability to cushion on impact.

Climate

The variables in climate that affect the runner are heat, humidity, cold, and altitude above sea level. Whether operating singly or collectively, they tend to impair running performance as they approach the extremes. More important, they may pose significant hazards to health. These potential hazards and the measures that can be taken to counteract them are discussed in the following sections.

Heat. Our bodies have very sensitive heat-regulating mechanisms, which, when they are allowed to function normally, maintain central body (core) temperature within a narrow range around the average value of 98.6°F. Two centers located at the base of the brain are responsible for this regulation. They are sensitive to the temperature of the blood reaching them and also to sensations transmitted to them through a special system of nerve pathways whose terminals are located in the skin. They control body temperature by regulating the flow of blood to different parts of the body and by modifying the sweat rate.

The external factors that affect the runner's maintaining heat balance are radiation, conduction, convection, and evaporation. In running outdoors, the amount of radiation depends on direct or indirect exposure to the sun; indoors it depends on the amount of heat generated by the heating apparatus and by the number of persons occupying the space. Conduction refers to the heat taken up by the body as the result of contact with a surface that has a temperature higher than the body temperature or lost by contact with a colder surface. In the case of a runner, this would be the shoes or the feet. Convection is the rate of air flow moving over the body of the runner. The air flow generated solely by the action of running is generally negligible compared with what may result from local wind conditions. Evaporation of water vapor occurs from both the lungs and the skin. At rest, most occurs from the lungs; but during running, evaporation of sweat from the skin is responsible for 95 percent or more of the body's ability to cool itself.

The body generates heat to maintain a normal core temperature. When exercising, a great deal more heat is generated than is needed, and the body must get rid of the excess. It can tolerate an increase of 4°F without much difficulty for hours at a time, but when internal temperature rises above 104°F, serious problems begin to arise. At 106°F the heat-regulating mechanisms tend to break down and internal temperature may then continue to rise rapidly until brain death occurs at somewhere between 108° and 110°F. Factors that can cause this breakdown in the exercising body are an excess of heat coming in from radiation and conduction, inadequate air flow over the body, and inability to evaporate sweat or produce it rapidly enough.

Running at the hotter times of the day, usually when the sun is high in the sky, may result in a net gain of heat by the body if the air temperature is higher than the core temperature of the exercising body. The nature and amount of clothing will affect this exchange: light-colored clothing will reflect a certain amount of the sun's radiation, whereas dark clothing will absorb it, and the unclothed body can radiate heat more effectively than the clothed one. Running in the shade of buildings or trees cuts down incoming radiation. A cloudy day does not necessarily offer protection since the ultraviolet radiation penetrates the clouds and the air temperature may be quite high.

A breeze is comfortable in hot weather because it facilitates radiation of heat as well as promoting evaporation. Its cooling effect at high temperatures depends on how much of the body surface is exposed. The evaporation of sweat, since it is by far the most important factor in cooling the body, should be encouraged in every way possible. This requires that sufficient areas of the skin be exposed, that enough water and salt be available to the body, and that the sweating apparatus be functioning normally. (Clothing for running was discussed in Chapter 4.) In hot weather, the lighter and looser the clothing, the better. When it is thoroughly soaked it should be changed if possible, because wet clothing covering the skin becomes a barrier to evaporation.

Making sufficient water available is the chief key to preventing heat cramps, heat exhaustion, and heat stroke. This is done principally by drinking plenty of water during the day, especially on hot days, and by taking water during long-distance races, say, 6 miles or longer. You don't have to worry about taking too much since researchers have shown that with water freely available and constant urging to drink, runners still will not come near replacing what they lose in sweat during a distance race.

You don't need fancy drinks laced with sugar and various salts. Indeed, you are better off without them. Unless the concentration of these substances is below what you ordinarily find in your blood, they delay the absorption of the water you need from the upper part of your intestine. If the concentration is very high, it will actually draw water out of your bloodstream into your intestinal tract. Alcoholic drinks, such as beer, which have been advocated by some runners who should know better, also have a tendency to cause dehydration, a further aggravation of your problem in hot weather.

If you are beginning your training in hot weather and are not fully accustomed to being out of doors, you may need to add a little ordinary table salt to your diet at mealtimes to avoid heat cramps. This should be necessary only for the first 2 or 3 weeks since your body reacts to repeated exercise by conserving salt and reducing the amount that appears in your urine by a factor of about 100.

Should you develop leg cramps while running in hot weather, don't try to run through them. Stop, rest, and drink some water until they go away. If you can add a little salt to it, so much the better. Remember that there are causes other than these of heat cramps; if they recur you should look into the other possibilities with your physician.

The signs of heat exhaustion are faintness, weakness, and mental confusion. If you feel these symptoms coming on, don't try to run through them. Stop and find some shade and some water. If you have been sweating heavily without feeling any of these symptoms and you notice that you are not sweating as much and your skin has become hot and dry, you are in the initial stage of heat stroke, the most dangerous of the body's responses to heat stress. You need to stop all activity and find a means to start cooling your body as rapidly as possible. Ice applied externally and taken internally will help; alcohol rubs with all your clothing removed, and other measures that can be taken by a medical team (if one is available), will keep you alive if they can be started promptly.

Although women on the average have a lower sweat rate than men, they don't seem to be any more susceptible to the various forms of heat stress. Perhaps the fact that men on average have a greater body mass, which makes it more difficult for them to radiate their body heat effectively, tends to counteract their ability to sweat more effectively.

Humidity. The relative humidity is important to the runner in hot weather because it affects the rate of evaporation of sweat from the body. Although you don't ordinarily think of severe heat stress occurring until the air temperature is over 80°F, heat stroke can occur at air temperatures as low as 65°F if the humidity is in the range of 90 percent.

The index used by the armed forces to determine when it is safe to carry out certain types of outdoor exercises combines the readings of the air temperature from a conventional thermometer taken in the shade, a globe thermometer that is painted black to absorb the direct rays of the sun, and a psychrometer, which is a wet-bulb thermometer that gives a reading indicating the relative humidity when it is exposed to a current of air. The index is composed of 0.1 of the reading of the standard thermometer; 0.2 of the reading of the globe thermometer; and 0.7 of the reading of the psychrometer. If you don't have a psychrometer, you can get the relative humidity reading for your area from the weather service at the nearest airport or from a local radio station. If the still air temperature is above 70°F and the relative humidity 80 percent or above, you would be wise to take only a short run and not get very far from help in case you need it. When the relative humidity is more than 90 percent, as it might be on a very warm, rainy day, you would be better off not to run any great distance but limit yourself to some limbering-up exercises and short sprints.

The relative humidity is of little importance to the runner in cold weather, except in one respect: The body will lose heat very rapidly on a cold day if clothing is wet. If under such circumstances you are unable to change into dry clothing and high humidity prevents drying of your clothing, you will be in much greater danger of suffering a severe reaction from cold stress.

Cold. Exposure of the body to severe cold may result in serious local or general reactions. The local chilling of body tissues to the point where cell death occurs is known as frostbite. The general chilling of the body to the point where core temperature falls more than a few degrees below the average temperature of 99°F is called hypothermia. In the extreme situation, frostbite can result in loss of body parts, such as fingers and toes; hypothermia can result in death.

When the skin is chilled by exposure to cold, it first becomes red, then purplish, and finally white. The sequence of events causing these color changes is an initial dilation of the capillaries in the skin in an attempt to keep it warm, slowing of the capillary circulation, and then closing down of the more superficial ones as the circulation is augmented in the deeper layers. In the red phase, there may be a slight stinging sensation in the skin; when it becomes purplish, the skin "burns"; and when it is white, there is an ache. This phase is sometimes known as "frost nip." If it becomes completely numb, you know that some tissue death—frostbite—has occurred.

Never try to rewarm skin suffering from cold effects by rubbing it vigorously, especially with snow. If some cell damage has already occurred, you will make it worse. If it hasn't, you may bring it on. Instead, cover it with something warm and soft and allow it to rewarm gradually. Fingers, for example, may be rewarmed by placing them in the armpits.

Some people are concerned about the effect of breathing in very cold air. If you have had a problem with coronary heart disease and have angina, breathing cold air may bring on an attack of pain, so you should wear a mask when outdoors in the cold. If you have a tendency to exercise-induced bronchospasm (EIB) or frank asthma, you may need a mask since cold air can set off severe breathing difficulty. Otherwise, your nose and throat should provide enough baffling to prevent your feeling any chest pain or discomfort from cold.

Hypothermia, a general lowering of the body temperature, is manifested at first by confusion and disorientation, followed by drowsiness, sleep, and eventually coma and death if resuscitation is not forthcoming. The onset is insidious, so it is better not to run any distance alone in very cold weather, especially out in the country. Two or three persons running together can watch one another for the first symptoms, such as inattention to conversation, remarks way off the subject, confusion about the route, and so on.

Survival has occurred following lowering of core temperature to an estimated 68°F, but internal temperatures below 80°F, if sustained for any period without life-support systems, are usually fatal. It is difficult to determine the temperature of a hypothermic person in the field, since special thermometers are necessary. If oral or rectal temperature falls below that which can be read on a regular clinical thermometer, the person needs to be placed under medical observation and treatment as quickly as possible.

Emergency treatment of hypothermia includes getting the exposed person into as warm a shelter as possible, changing any wet clothing, and covering the person with everything available that is warm and dry. A sleeping bag is good if available. If it has room for two, a person who is not affected should get in with the hypothermic individual to transfer as much body heat as possible. In the meantime, arrangements should be made for transfer to the nearest hospital or medical facility as quickly as possible. Don't waste time with rewarming at the scene if transportation is available.

There is some danger of death from "rewarming shock," which produces cardiac arrest, if the knowledge and materials to prevent it are not available. Some evidence suggests that this shock can be avoided by rewarming the body from the inside out rather than outside in with inserted tubes through which warm water is circulated into the stomach and lower bowel.

Reduced Barometric Pressure. As your altitude above sea level increases, the air becomes thinner. The resultant decrease in the partial pressure of oxygen at altitudes as low as 4,000 feet may cause you to become unusually short of breath on exertion such as running. At 7,000 feet, you may not be able to run any distance at all until you become accustomed (acclimated) to the change in atmospheric pressure. At 10,000 feet it may be very difficult to train at all, and above 12,000 feet even walking can be a problem. Above 15,000 feet, unless you are an experienced mountaineer, you will need supplemental oxygen, but you won't expect to be running at that altitude. The highest level at which any running competition takes place is at La Paz, Bolivia, which is somewhat above 10,000 feet in the Andes mountains, where the Bolivian games are held.

Ordinarily, the hemoglobin in the red corpuscles in your blood is close to 99 percent saturated with oxygen. Unless you are in an atmosphere where oxygen is low, there will also be some oxygen dissolved in the blood plasma. You can still function fairly well for many activities when this saturation is decreased slightly, but any skilled performance, whether mental or physical, is reduced. Your body reacts to this situation in a number of ways, but the most significant is by increasing the number of red corpuscles, and thereby increasing the hemoglobin carrying capacity of your blood.

This change takes time—on the average, about 3 weeks —to return you to your ability to function as well as at sea level. No matter how long you stay up at altitude you won't be able to equal your best sea-level running time at any distance of a mile or more. On the other hand, because of the increased hemoglobin in the blood, you may be able to run somewhat faster than normal for a little while when you return to sea level. Then your hemoglobin comes back in a few weeks to its normal level. There is some evidence to indicate that training for three weeks at altitude, coming down to sea level for 1 week and continuing training, and then going back to train at altitude for another 3 weeks is effective.

In recent years, Ethiopia and Kenya have produced the most outstanding long-distance runners in the world, who were born, reared, and trained in the highlands of those countries. These men never seem to lose their advantage even when they stay for relatively long periods at sea level. Many other world-class runners now spend some time every year training at altitudes from 7,000 to 8,000 feet and feel that it helps them. Jim Ryun set his world record for the mile and 1,500-meter runs after a period of training in the Rocky Mountains.

One thing you will notice if you run at moderate altitude is that you get thirsty very easily and will need to drink much more water. This is because the vapor pressure of water is also lower than at sea level. Relative humidity may get very high, however, in some tropical or semi-tropical areas, such as Mexico City, during rainy seasons.

If you are going to a moderate altitude to run a race and are not acclimated, the best thing to do is to go as late as possible before the race: The effect on your performance will be less in the first 24 hours than in the next 3 days. The low point of performance is reached on the third day after arriving at altitude.

Mountain sickness can start for some people at altitudes as low as 3,500 feet. It is characterized by headache, general malaise, loss of appetite, and difficulty in sleeping. These symptoms will usually clear in 4 to 5 days. At around 10,000 feet, you may run into a more serious problem—pulmonary edema; that is, the blood becomes congested in the lungs, reducing your breathing capacity even further. Treatment with oxygen is required, and you should return to sea level as soon as possible. Very young and very old persons are most susceptible to this condition, if they travel rapidly, as by airplane, to such an altitude.

If you are a smoker, you are going to have a greater problem at a higher altitude. The carbon monoxide from the smoke will displace oxygen from the hemoglobin, since hemoglobin has a 200-times-greater affinity for carbon monoxide than for oxygen.

If you are interested only in running sprints and distances of 800 meters or less, you may find some improvement in your running times at higher altitudes, because air resistance is lower and gravitational pull on your body is decreased slightly. Even so, you can still improve your ability to train and to run repeated sprints by becoming acclimated to altitude.

Diet

Your internal environment is as important as your external environment. Your diet plays a big part in determining this internal environment. In Chapter 2 we discussed the metabolic factors relating to running and described the roles played by carbohydrates, fats, and proteins. Now we will talk about how to ensure that adequate supplies of these essential nutrients can be made available to you in your diet.

There are no mysteries about good nutrition for the runner, no matter what you may have heard or read. New diets appear almost every month, it seems, and disappear almost as quickly. Most are harmless variations on a standard diet, but some are dangerous to health and should be avoided. The so-called liquid protein and zen macrobiotic diets are good examples of the latter.

When you were in high school or college, you were exposed at some time or other to the concept of the "well-balanced" diet, composed of five basic food groups. This concept is still accepted as valid by the real authorities in nutrition. What is good for everybody is also good for the runner. (This diet is described in the table in Chapter 2.)

The total number of calories (usually expressed as kilo calories) that you will need per day or per week if you are running regularly can be calculated by keeping a careful record of your daily activities, including the time you spend running and your average pace, and consulting a table that shows the energy costs for all these activities. In practice, you don't need to do this if you will simply keep a daily record of your weight before running. (It should be before, since dehydration will vary according to many factors related to your workout for a given day.)

If you haven't been running or exercising regularly, you can expect that you will lose weight during the first 2 to 3 months after you begin. This represents chiefly a loss of available body fat. It will be somewhat less than your total fat loss because you will add some lean body weight in the form of muscle. When you reach this point, your weight should stabilize and change little more than 1 to 2 pounds from day to day. If it remains stable, you know that you are taking in enough calories to supply your body's needs for your daily activities as well as your running. A severe cold or temporary intestinal upset might throw it off for a few days, however.

You may have heard about "carbohydrate loading" by long-distance runners. The principle behind this is that although fat is the principal source of energy during a long-distance run, you also continue to burn available carbohydrate stores. If at some point in the race you wish to increase your pace or finish with a strong "kick," you need glycogen.

Experiments in Sweden that involved sampling stores of glycogen from the thigh muscles before and after exhaustive exercise showed that persons eating a diet that was very high in carbohydrates for 1 week before a hard test run on an exercise bicycle could build up their stores of glycogen to double the amount that would normally accumulate from a well-balanced diet. In the test run itself, they could keep riding half again as long as those who had eaten balanced meals.

It was also observed that if muscle glycogen stores were completely exhausted and the subjects were fed a low-carbohydrate diet for the next 3 days, muscle stores of glycogen increased even more and they could ride the exercise bicycle twice as long before they were exhausted.

Several questions were not answered by these experiments, however. One of these was the question of how often this dietary trick could be successfully repeated. Since storing glycogen requires adding extra body water, it means a temporary increase in body weight. Although this has an advantage in making more water available to prevent dehydration, the extra few pounds might be a handicap to the highly trained runner during the early part of a race.

For the average recreational runner who is not involved in serious competition, there does not seem to be any great advantage to carbohydrate loading. It is enough to remember that carbohydrate is an important energy source and to get enough of it, particularly in the last week before a race. Don't neglect the importance of protein for replacement of muscle, blood, and hormones. Keep in mind that cereals, including bread and pasta, are the best sources of carbohydrate gram for gram of any food, and they are second only to meat, fish, eggs and dairy products as sources of protein.

This answers in part the question of whether a runner can satisfy energy and other nutritional requirements on a strict vegetarian diet. The answer is yes. It requires some imagination in food preparation to keep it from becoming boring, however. It can supply the runner's needs for vitamins as well. (Make certain that your diet is rich in legumes, the source of B-12, an essential vitamin not found in other vegetables or fruits.) In fact, because the diet includes so many vegetables and fruits, and because almost all our cereals are fortified with vitamins, vegetarians are seldom in need of vitamin supplements.

Who needs vitamin supplementation if he or she is eating a well-balanced diet? Virtaully no one, unless the person has a special problem in absorbing certain vitamins (as in the disease called pernicious anemia), or is convalescing from surgery or serious acute illness and has not been able to eat properly. It is true that increased amounts of vita mins of the B complex and C are used by the muscles during exercise, but amounts in excess of those in your regular diet—if it is well balanced—are not necessary. If you take extra quantities of these water-soluble vitamins, they are not stored but simply excreted in the urine. Vitamin B_{12} injections have been popular with some runners. Your daily requirement for this vitamin is about 6 micrograms, but some athletes are taking as much as 1,000 micrograms.

Timing of meals can be important for a runner. Most persons will be more comfortable if they haven't eaten for about 3 hours before running. If you feel that you have to ingest something in the last hour or two before you run, take something liquid that will be easily digested. Don't eat candy bars or drink beverages with a high sugar content, because about the time you start running your blood sugar may take a sharp drop and this will make it difficult for your muscles to get the glucose they need.

Steer clear of exotic substances, such as bee pollen, another favorite of some runners. They are expensive and don't offer anything to help you in spite of high-powered advertising and great word-of-mouth praise. When the great Australian runner Herb Elliot was supposedly eating only the nuts and dried-fruit diet prescribed by his coach, Percy Cerutty, he was in truth eating anything he pleased when the coach wasn't looking.

Drugs

If you are taking some medication prescribed by a physician on a regular basis, ask if it will have any effect on your ability to run or if you should change the dose or the schedule. Drugs such as propranolol, which are prescribed for the control of angina and regulation of heart irregularities, may also slow the heart rate so much that running becomes difficult.

If you are a diabetic, it is especially important to review your running program with your physician and get his or her advice about regulating your condition. This is particularly true if you are taking insulin. The location of your injection is important when you are exercising, since muscle activity in that area increases the rate of absorption of insulin and may throw you into insulin shock. The best site for injection in the athlete is in the lower part of the abdomen because muscle activity is least there in most sports.

Most insulin-dependent diabetics find that their insulin requirement is lower on days when they exercise. But since they usually tend to eat more if they are taking vigorous exercise, they may find that the insulin requirement may not vary much from that on non-exercise days. Monitoring your urine is always important if you are a diabetic, but when you are also a runner it is even more important. On days when you find a positive acetone test, it is better not to run; consult your physician to have him explain why this is so.

Many runners are interested in knowing if there is any drug that will make them better runners. No such drug exists. Caffeine has an interesting effect on mobilizing fatty acids in the blood, which in some laboratory tests has appeared to help in long-distance running. Moderate amounts, such as are present in coffee and tea, are all that are necessary to produce this effect. Taking too much may cause a tense, nervous state that could interfere with running performance.

Amphetamines are not only useless to the runner but may interfere with the delicate balance of coordination that has been established in training. Anabolic steroids are also useless as aids to performance, despite the fondness that some Eastern European coaches and weight lifters seem to have for them.

If you were a smoker of tobacco when you started running, the chances are that you have stopped before reading this. The reason is that you are, or have been, too much bothered by the double handicap that smoking imposes on your running. The hot smoke causes a constriction of your bronchial passages, which cuts down on the amount of oxygen you can deliver per minute from your lungs to your muscles. This amount is further reduced by the carbon monoxide from the smoke, which monopolizes some of the hemoglobin that would otherwise be carrying oxygen.

Nicotine is a very toxic substance, but it creates a powerful addiction in some persons. You will see some smokers who run, but they do so at a considerable sacrifice of their potential achievements in time and distance. If you give up smoking you will gradually recover much, if not all, of the lung function you had sacrificed. How much depends on how long and how much you smoked. Smoking marijuana has effects similar to smoking tobacco.

Alcohol contains calories in the form of carbohydrates, but if taken just before or during a run, very few of these calories are available as an energy source, since the liver has to convert the alcohol to glycogen and this takes time. Alcohol depresses the central nervous system and slows complex reaction times so that its overall effect on running performance is negative. If taken in any large quantity the night before a race, its effects the next day can be devastating. Taken during a race, it acts as a diuretic and simply increases dehydration. If the day is hot and humid, it will help bring on heat exhaustion much earlier.

Cocaine is not helpful to a runner, in spite of its ability to stimulate the central nervous system. It is an extremely toxic drug and can cause anaphylactic shock and death in a few minutes in persons who are sensitive to it. Other street drugs cause either so much disorientation or depression that they are positively detrimental to the runner.

6.
running injuries—
how they happen
and what to do
about them

"THE RUNNER RUNS IN PAIN" has long been a maxim of track coaches, reflecting both the physical pain that invariably results from hard physiologic work, and the psychic consequences of concentration, exertion, and exhaustion. Some amount of pain will always accompany running. How much depends on a number of variables—the runner's perception and tolerance of pain, age, physical condition, and extent of exertion.

Yet one cause of pain—and disability—that every runner hopes to minimize is injury. Running and, at the very least, aches and soreness are inseparable, and by looking at the body's structure and what running demands of it, you'll appreciate why.

Begin by stripping away the skin and muscles: Imagine the skeleton that used to stand in the biology classroom, and see it in the motions of running—making those small leaps, landing from each on the heel alone with a force of around 2½ times the runner's body weight at a rate of several thousand blows to the heel per mile. Obviously, the skeleton is subjected to crunch after crunch as force is transmitted from the heel up the leg bones through the bony girdle that forms the pelvis and into the spinal column. This force of impact likewise puts considerable stress on cartilage, the gristly, shock-absorbing tissue that lines the joints and forms the disks that separate the vertebrae of the spine. Thus, any structural or functional defect, particularly in that key extremity—the foot—may cause symptoms and disability. Even if the problem was not apparent in walking, the greatly increased stress of running may bring it to light.

Wrapping the skeleton with its muscles, ligaments, tendons, and other tissues that give it stability and movement, the feet, ankles, legs, knees, thighs, hips, and spine become interdependent parts of a coordinated system. The movement of one part through its possible range of motion causes some action or reaction in the other parts, and when the weight of the body is supported partially or wholly by the system, the failure of one component to move properly produces some strain or misalignment in the others. The initial symptom may appear in a part that is affected only secondarily. Pain in the knee, for example, may actually be caused by a problem in the foot or back.

Seeing or experiencing the body in running movement, one can appreciate the inordinate stress applied to the tissues that bind the system together, as they must both support and propel the body through its range of motions.

Besides the physical stress invariably caused by running, a number of other internal factors may influence injury. These include your body type, bone structure, weight, level of conditioning, fatigue, coordination, sense of balance, and level of skill. Some of these, of course, are built in by nature, and you must do the best you can with the structure you've been given.

External factors can be critical, too, and may often be the sole cause of injury. The running surface; fit and condition of shoes and socks; frequency, duration, and intensity of running; and failure to warm up or cool down properly all can contribute to musculoskeletal damage.

Let's examine some of the potential running injuries, their causes, symptoms, and signs, and recommended treatment measures.

The Foot

Without question, the foot is the most frequent site of injury in runners. Considering that each foot has 26 bones, 19 muscles, and 107 ligaments, and that the feet bear the runner's body weight at each stride, this shouldn't be surprising.

Sprains, dislocations, and fractures of the toes can be caused by stubbing the toes while running barefoot, jamming the toes, or having them stepped on. The affected toe or toes become painful, stiff, tender to the touch, and perhaps deformed.

In the case of a sprain, the affected toe should be taped to one of the adjoining toes; the runner will be disabled for 2 to 5 days. A sprained great toe should be splinted and rested.

A dislocated small toe should be reduced (set) and taped to the next toe for 3 to 7 days. A dislocated great toe, however, should be X-rayed for a possible fracture, reduced, and a splint applied. Surgery may be required for removal of a bone fragment and repair of the ligament, so a dislocation of the great toe could disable a runner for 3 weeks to 3 months.

A fracture of a small toe should be reduced by taping or splinting, while a great-toe fracture requires reduction and application of a non-weight-bearing cast for 3 weeks and a weight-bearing cast for 3 weeks. Total disability for a toe fracture may range from 1 to 12 weeks.

Metatarsal sprain may be caused by landing off balance or wearing shoes that do not provide adequate support. Pain, along with swelling and tenderness, is felt across the arch. Resting the foot, and perhaps applying supportive tape, is the recommended treatment. Disability is usually 2 to 4 weeks.

Achilles tendinitis, or inflammation of the tendon, is one of the most common injuries in runners. Nearly every runner suffers it to some degree, particularly the beginner. It may result from chronic strain, poorly fitted shoes, or extreme pronation of the feet. The tendon becomes painful, swollen, and tender to the touch, and the best thing the runner can do is rest and, later, correct problems related to the shoes or the running position of the feet. Meanwhile, a physician may prescribe an anti-inflammatory drug or even recommend surgery if the tendon problem is chronic. However, prevention is far better than treatment—appropriate stretching exercises before and after running are crucial to minimizing injury of the Achilles tendon.

Plantar fasciitis, another common form of inflammation, affects the ligaments in the sole of the foot where they join the heel. Chronic strain, poor foot positioning, or improper shoes may be responsible for the pain that arises along the sole and heel. Putting a rubber "doughnut" under the heel, using a shoe with a heel lift and a stiff shank, and adjusting the running position of the feet may solve the problem with a minimal period of disability. In resistant cases it may be necessary to separate the fascia surgically from its attachment to the heel bone.

Heel spur, a bony growth on the heel, is usually associated with plantar fasciitis. Resting the foot, being sure shoes are correctly fitted, and perhaps using an orthotic device will usually solve the problem, but disability may range from 3 to 6 weeks. Removal of the spur is not curative and may aggravate the symptoms by making the fascia tighter.

Hemorrhaging under the toenails can result from nails that are too long or from poorly fitted shoes or both. Constantly striking the nails against the front of the shoe can cause bleeding under one or more nails, resulting in pain and discoloration. The nail should be punctured with a sterile sharp object to release the blood. The runner may be disabled 1 to 3 days, and the nail may eventually drop off. Such hemorrhage is preventable by keeping the nails trimmed and wearing shoes that fit properly. The tip of the big toe should not be closer to the tip of the shoe than the breadth of your thumb.

Hammer toe is caused by a contraction of the tendon which extends the toe, pulling up the first joint while the second and third joints bend downwards toward the sole of the foot. As a result, a painful callus develops over the tip of the toe as well as on the dorsal aspect of the involved joints. A callus also may arise under the head of the deformed toe. The disorder is caused by poorly fitted shoes or inherently short flexor tendons. Spacious, well-padded shoes may relieve the painful calluses, although surgical correction may be required for serious deformity. Recovery from surgery may take 3 weeks.

Morton's neuroma refers to a small tumor that develops from a nerve between the toes, usually the third and fourth toes. The tumor causes pain in the metatarsus, which can be relieved in some runners by use of an arch support that reduces pressure and allows the inflammation to resolve. However, it may be necessary to remove the tumor surgically.

Corns usually are caused by shoes that fit poorly. These painful calluses are very sensitive to pressure, and they can usually be relieved by having a physician pare them down with a scalpel and by wearing shoes that fit properly.

Blisters, a very common affliction of runners, should be prevented rather than treated. Here are some useful tips: Apply alcohol to the feet before running; powder the feet after the alcohol has dried; wear clean, dry socks; break in new shoes gradually; apply adhesive tape over areas of the feet that are vulnerable to blistering; and, during hot weather, coat the feet with petroleum jelly and wear ventilated running shoes.

If a blister should form, puncture it at the edge with a sterile needle, apply gentle pressure to drain the fluid, and put on a sterile dressing and pad.

Hallux valgus, the condition in which the great toe bends toward and over the adjoining toe, probably begins as a hereditary tendency that is aggravated by improperly fitted shoes. It causes pain, swelling, and tenderness at the base of the toe. Correcting the fit of the shoes and applying a splint to the metatarsal often relieves the symptoms, although surgical correction may be necessary. An operation usually means 4 to 6 months of disability.

Metatarsal fracture may be caused by chronic strain, landing off balance on the foot, or poorly fitted shoes. Pain occurs in the metatarsal when weight is applied to the foot, and the area above the arch is tender to the touch. The fracture must be treated by reduction, application of a cast, and rest, with a disability of 8 to 12 weeks.

Sesamoid bones, the small, nodular bones that are located in a tendon or joint capsule, are subject to bruising because of improper shoes or chronic strain. The injury causes pain, with redness, tenderness, and swelling over the plantar region of the great toe. Recommended treatment includes rest, properly fitted shoes, and perhaps an anti-inflammatory drug. Disability ranges from 3 to 6 weeks.

Bursitis in runners' feet occurs around the calcaneus, the heel bone. Usually caused by poorly fitted shoes or an abnormal tilt of the calcaneus itself, the inflammation is quite painful and disabling. It is generally treated by injection of an anesthetic or steroid drug. Some runners may require surgical removal of a bony prominence from the calcaneus.

Morton's foot is not actually an injury but a rather common variation of the structure of the foot, which was described by the anatomist Dr. Dudley Morton some years ago. It has had a great deal of publicity among runners because it may—but does not necessarily—create foot pain. Dr. Morton was interested in this variation because he felt that it was a throwback to a more primitive type of foot structure, such as is found among the larger anthropoid apes. He would be very much surprised at the notoriety his discovery has gained so many years later.

The essence of this structural variation is a short first metatarsal that is separated from the second metatarsal by more than the usual space, a separation that extends back between the tarsal bones that lie immediately behind it. Since a major share of the weight placed on the forefoot in walking and running ordinarily falls on the outer end, or head, of the first metatarsal, the consequence of this short metatarsal is that the head of the second metatarsal becomes more prominent and has to bear a greater proportion than normal of the body weight. If you look at the sole of your foot, you should see a rather heavy callus behind the great toe, where the weight is normally borne. If you have a Morton-type foot, you will see that this callus lies over the head of the second metatarsal. Don't assume that you have such a foot simply because the second toe sticks out farther than the great toe—this can be normal.

The second metatarsal is not as large and well developed for weight-bearing as the first. The callus that forms over it will be smaller and may become chronically painful and very tender to pressure. Relief can be obtained only by placing a pad under the short head of the first metatarsal (or building this correction into an orthotic) so that it becomes more prominent and takes the strain from the second metatarsal.

Because the first and second metatarsal heads are widely separated in this condition, the transverse metatarsal arch may be weaker than normal and have more of a tendency to flatten under pressure. This may be a reason for the use of an orthotic, which can help make up for this deficiency.

Peroneal tendinitis results from chronic strain and extreme pronation of the feet. Pain and tenderness are felt on the side of the foot and the peroneal tendons themselves are swollen. Resting the foot is essential, and a physician may prescribe an oral anti-inflammatory drug or inject a steroid around the tendon. Disability ranges from 2 to 6 weeks.

Tarsal fractures can occur from the chronic stress of running or from a direct blow. Pain usually is located in the center of the foot, with tenderness and swelling over the affected bone. If the fracture is not displaced, disability may range up to 10 weeks. The runner must avoid putting weight on the foot, and after 4 to 6 weeks a walking cast can be applied. If the fracture is displaced, it must be reduced and the foot placed in a cast. Disability may range up to 24 weeks.

Athlete's foot is a fungus infection of the skin of the foot caused by one of the several species of dermatophytes, especially *Epidermophyton floccosum* and *Trichophyton rubrum*. Although it commonly involves the skin between the toes, it may involve any part of the skin of the foot. When it involves the toenails it is very difficult to eliminate.

The growth of this fungus is favored by warmth and

moisture. This breaks down the natural surface barrier and allows the fungus to invade the skin. The symptoms are itching and burning, and the skin presents a moist, macerated, reddened appearance, often with loose patches of dead, whitened skin. If secondary infection occurs, the toes or foot may become generally reddened and swollen. Red streaks running from the top of the foot up the leg indicate spread of the infection into the lymphatics.

Treatment includes drying the involved area, removing dead patches of skin, and applying any of the several antifungal ointments or creams on the market. Desenex® ointment, Tinactin® solution or cream, Enzactin® cream, and Halotex® cream and solution all may be effective for local application. Your physician or dermatologist can advise which is best for you.

If the nails are involved, your physician will prescribe Grisactin® in tablet form. This medication must be taken until the infected nails grow out completely, usually a matter of months.

Prevention is accomplished by keeping the feet as dry as possible, changing socks frequently if you wear them, spraying an antifungal powder (any of the aforementioned name brands) into your shoes, and avoiding rubbing too briskly with the towel between the toes after a bath or shower, since this breaks down the skin's barrier to infection. Persons whose feet perspire excessively may have to take other measures recommended by their physicians.

The Ankle

Sprains and Achilles tendon strain and rupture are the most common injuries that affect the ankle. Sprains most often result from running on uneven surfaces—"I twisted my ankle" is the most common complaint, and it's literally true. Symptoms may range from a mild ache to severe pain and inability to put weight on the ankle. Thus, severity of sprains varies widely, but treatment basically amounts to keeping weight off the ankle until swelling begins to decline, taping it for support, and returning to full running only when there is no longer any swelling or tenderness. However, if a sprain results in a complete rupture of a ligament, surgical repair may be necessary, followed by up to 12 weeks of recovery.

The Achilles tendon, connecting as it does the large muscle of the calf to the ankle, is subject to continual stress in runners, which may result in small tears or even complete rupture of the tendon. In the latter case, the tendon is severely painful and will not tolerate any weight on the foot. Surgery is mandatory and disability may range up to 6 months.

When the tendon is inflamed, treatment is aimed first at reducing the inflammation. This can be done by rest, switching workouts to every other day, avoiding hills, running on a soft surface, and perhaps using a heel lift in the shoe. Aspirin and medications such as Butazolidin® (phenylbutazone) or Tandearil® (oxyphenbutazone) can be taken in tablet form to relieve the inflammation.

Prevention of Achilles tendon problems is far better than treatment, and this can be accomplished by religiously performing stretching exercises before and after running (see figures at the end of this chapter) and by increasing one's running program very gradually. Wearing sturdy running shoes with a rounded, stable flared heel, plus an

Achilles tendon protector and a strong heel counter, is also extremely helpful.

Inflammation of the extensor tendons is another ankle-related injury caused by chronic strain. Pain along the instep and swelling and tenderness over the extensor tendons are characteristic of the injury. Treatment amounts to resting and taking anti-inflammatory drugs. Disability may range up to 3 weeks.

Retrocalcaneal Achilles bursitis is a term that refers to inflammation and pain at the point where the Achilles tendon attaches to the heel. Treatment is aimed at reducing pressure on the heel from the shoe, and a heel lift may do the trick. In some cases, the physician may elect to inject an anti-inflammatory drug around the tendon to relieve symptoms.

Posterior tibial tendinitis is another common overuse injury in runners. Long runs on uneven surfaces with inadequate foot support may result in pain along the back of the tibia. Running on high-crown roads without switching sides and poor foot position also may contribute to the disorder, which may be managed by a change in workout patterns, application of ice, and anti-inflammatory drugs. A well-fitted arch support, orthotic device, or heel wedge can be very effective in prevention.

Stress fractures can be brought on by chronic strain of running. Such a fracture is marked by pain in the involved bone and tenderness over the fracture site. The best treatment is to refrain from running (although normal walking is permitted) for 6 to 8 weeks. X rays may not reveal the fine line of the fracture until bone callus appears in the process of healing.

The Leg

Among the disorders that afflict the runner's legs, shin splints are perhaps the most common. Although the term is often used to describe any discomfort in the leg, shin splints are defined by the American Medical Association as "pain and discomfort in the leg from repetitive running on hard surfaces, or forcible, extensive use of the foot flexors." The diagnosis should be limited to muscle-tendon inflammation, says the AMA guide, and should not include a fatigue fracture or circulatory disorder.

Shin splints seem to be an inflammatory disorder caused by overuse of the lower leg muscles, and tend to affect beginners, particularly when they run more than they should.

Pain along the shin usually begins at the onset of the workout and is aggravated by exercise. The muscles of the lower leg become tender and the leg may be stiff after it is rested. Treatment includes rest, application of ice, anti-inflammatory drugs, and taping or strapping. Stretching before and after running is helpful in prevention, and checking the shoes for proper condition and fit is also important to reduce the risk of shin splints.

Muscle strains and ruptures of the leg muscles are other possible accidents that can occur in runners. Imbalance between opposing muscle groups, sudden forced contraction, and inadequate warm-up may all contribute to muscle strain, which is marked by pain, tenderness, and weakness in the involved muscle. Resting the injured muscle and undergoing a program of strengthening exercises are recommended for treatment and prevention. Disability may range up to 4 weeks.

Tendinitis, a result of recurrent or chronic strain, is another painful affliction of runners' legs. Besides the Achilles tendon, which has already been discussed, the popliteal tendon (the one behind the knee) is also subject to inflammation, although less frequently than its counterpart at the ankle. It may cause 2 to 4 weeks' disability and should be treated with rest and anti-inflammatory drugs.

Stress fracture is another strain-related leg problem in runners. This is most likely to occur in the tibia or the fibula, with pain during exercise and tenderness localized in the affected bone. Such a fracture may not show up on an X ray at the time of injury. Often the occurrence of stress fracture is revealed some time later by the presence of new bone tissue on the X-ray film. Meanwhile, the runner must give up that form of exercise for 6 to 8 weeks, and try to keep fit by swimming or riding an exercise bicycle.

Compartment syndrome is a term being used increasingly by sports medicine professionals. The "compartment" refers to one or more of the lower leg muscles, which are enclosed—much like a sausage—in a sheath of thin, tough tissue called fascia. The term itself refers to a condition in which the circulation and function of a muscle are compromised by increased pressure within the compartment.

At first the condition was thought to be rare; now, however, medical investigators suspect that the syndrome may not be rare in occurrence, but rather rarely diagnosed. With the increased popularity of running in recent years, physicians and trainers are becoming more alert to the possibility of compartment syndrome.

Although the problem has several types and causes, in runners the compartment syndrome stems from vigorous exercise, which increases muscle bulk and, hence, pressure within the compartments of the legs when the muscle swells further during the course of exercise.

The amount of pressure required to produce a compartmental syndrome in a given individual depends on a number of variables—duration of the period of pressure elevation, the condition of the tissues, and the local tissue pressure. Nevertheless, if pressure rises too high and is not reduced through natural processes, the runner may experience loss of sensation and weakness, swelling, and tenderness in the affected muscle, along with pain on flexing the foot or the toes.

When the compartment syndrome becomes acute, it is a surgical emergency: The fascia should be opened as soon as possible to relieve the intra-compartmental pressure. Moreover, the few studies to date have shown that the extent of permanent damage and loss of function is directly related to the lapse of time between onset of symptoms and surgical operation. When pain is recurrent with exercise but doesn't reach the stage where emergency surgery is required, slitting the fascial envelope covering the muscles involved as an elective surgical procedure may be curative.

In short, compartment syndrome can be a serious problem leading to permanent disability and even systemic illness if it is not managed promptly.

The Knee

As a single, albeit complex unit, the knee ranks with the foot as a frequent site of pain and injury. In fact, the term "runner's knee" has joined "tennis elbow" and "swimmer's shoulder" as one of the catch-all complaints among athletes.

Essentially, knee injuries generally result from the chronic strain of running, although occasionally a twisting-type injury or an inherent musculoskeletal defect may be responsible. Moreover, problems at other sites may actually cause symptoms in the knee. Improper positioning of the foot and leg, ill-fitting shoes, or running on hard surfaces can cause pain and injury in the knee.

Probably the most common problem is the one called chondromalacia patellae, which means literally softening of the cartilage of the kneecap. Although it is more likely to occur in teenagers than in adults, the disorder may be the result of poor alignment of the lower leg, poor running technique, an uneven running surface, a structural defect, or weakness of the quadriceps muscle. Whatever the cause of the misalignment, the kneecap does not track properly in its groove and the resulting irritation can cause softening and fragmentation of the cartilage on the posterior surface of the kneecap, with pain in and around the knee and tenderness on compression of the kneecap.

Treatment of chondromalacia includes resting the leg, applying ice, and doing isometric or weight-resistance exercises, limited to the last 30° of extension of the leg on the knee, to strengthen the quadriceps. Occasionally a cast may be necessary to immobilize the knee temporarily, and, in acute cases, surgery may be called for to remove loose fragments of cartilage and correct the positioning of the kneecap. Disability varies with conservative treatment, while after surgery it may range up to 12 weeks.

The knee has 14 bursae, any of which may become inflamed with the stress and friction of running. The inflammation causes considerable pain, which is relieved by injection of an anti-inflammatory drug into the involved bursa, application of ice, and, of course, resting the leg.

Tendinitis is a potential hazard for runners' knees just as it is for other sites. A result of chronic strain, the inflammation causes pain and tenderness in the involved tendon, as well as disability. Treatment consists of rest, oral anti-inflammatory drugs, and, in some cases, injection of a steroid drug near the tendon. Convalescence varies from 2 to 4 weeks.

Sprained ligaments also occur in and around the knee, perhaps because of twisting of the lower leg and knee. Such a sprain causes pain, tenderness, and swelling that can be treated by rest and progressive resistance exercise of the quadriceps. Surgery, however, may be required if a ligament is completely ruptured, in which case recovery time may be as long as 6 months.

Tearing a meniscus, one of the crescent-shaped disks of cartilage at the top of the tibia, is a serious and painful injury that may require surgical removal of all or a part of the torn meniscus, with a period of disability of 1 to 3 months. Such an injury usually results from direct force or torque (twisting pressure) applied to the knee.

Partial dislocation of the kneecap (patellar subluxation), caused by a weakness in the quadriceps, abnormal placement of the patellar tendon, or an unusual size or placement of the kneecap, may result in knee pain and swelling and some degree of disability. Isometric exercises to strengthen the quadriceps can help overcome the problem, but if symptoms persist surgery may be necessary, followed by up to 6 months' convalescence.

The Thigh

Fortunately for distance runners, they are less prone to thigh injuries than sprinters and other athletes who habitually put sudden, excessive stress on the legs. Even so, runners can suffer muscle strain and rupture, often because of disproportionate strength in the hamstring muscle as opposed to the quadriceps. Such a problem is best prevented by performing stretching exercises before and after running and by exercising to strengthen the quadriceps. Should strain occur, it is marked by pain in the thigh, and it can be treated by rest, elevating the leg, and applying ice and a compression bandage. Complete muscle rupture, on the other hand, may require surgical repair with up to 20 weeks' disability.

Tendinitis also can be a problem in the thigh. Its symptoms are the typical pain on running or walking and tenderness and swelling of the involved tendon. Resting the limb and taking an anti-inflammatory drug are recommended, and sometimes an injection around the tendon may be therapeutic. The disability period varies from 2 to 4 weeks but usually the tendinitis heals without a residual defect.

Bursitis with its characteristic pain, tenderness, and swelling can arise in the medial or lateral aspect of the thigh as well as in other areas. Rest and injection of an anesthetic and an anti-inflammatory drug are the usual treatment steps; disability ranges from 2 to 4 weeks.

Chronic strain of running can also cause a stress fracture of the femur (thigh bone). It is marked by pain in the bone itself, and resting the limb for 6 to 8 weeks is the only treatment.

The Hip

Although it is infrequent in runners, bursitis can occur at the upper end of the femur, where it joins the hip. It may be related to the stress of running, or to unequal length of the lower extremities. In this case, a heel lift and a slight reduction in the amount of running may overcome the problem. Meanwhile, rest and injections of a local anesthetic and an anti-inflammatory agent are recommended for treating the inflammation.

Osteochondritis, a disorder that involves inflammation of both bone and cartilage, can occur in runners, with hip pain and damage to the involved substances. Rest is the treatment for less serious cases, while more severe osteochondritis requires surgical repair and a convalescence of 16 to 20 weeks.

The Pelvis

Stress fracture of the pubic bone can occur as the result of chronic strain in runners, with sharp pain in the bone on attempting to run. As for all stress fractures, rest is the best medicine, in this case for about 6 to 8 weeks.

The Lower Back

Back pain is probably more common than hip and thigh problems in runners. At the outset, any derangement of the spinal disks or degenerative changes in the spine will be aggravated by running. In addition, the lower back is subject to its own strain, sprains, and stress fractures.

The lower back muscles can be strained by an imbalance between them and the abdominal muscles, by poor running technique, or by unequal length of the legs. Low-back pain is the result. Rest, application of cold packs, exercise to correct muscular imbalance, plus a heel lift for the shorter extremity are recommended treatment; the pain can be disabling for 2 to 4 weeks or even longer.

The same circumstances, as well as taking a fall, may also be responsible for a sprain of the lumbar ligaments, which results in low back pain that radiates into the buttocks and down the leg (sciatic pain). Correcting faults in running technique, particularly excessive lordosis, resting, and using a heel lift in the case of a short leg usually will correct the disorder, although disability may range up to 6 weeks.

A stress fracture in the spine can result from a twisting-type injury or from falling. Low-back and sciatic pain are the major symptoms. They can be treated with rest and a lumbo-sacral canvas support. Full recovery may take 8 to 12 weeks.

A fall or other inordinate trauma can also cause a rupture of a spinal disk. Besides low-back and sciatic pain, the injury is marked by weakness in one leg. With rest and support of the lower back, disability may amount to 8 weeks. Serious rupture, however, may require surgery, with a recovery time of up to 16 weeks.

Stitch in the side, another common complaint among runners, is a crampy pain in the abdomen, usually high on the right side under the ribs but sometimes in the upper mid-section or even low in the left side between the hip and the umbilicus. It appears sometimes after running just a short distance, and the pain can be so severe that the runner doubles over and has to stop. In some persons it is mild, however, and the victim can "run through" the discomfort. After stopping running the pain will usually pass spontaneously in a few minutes. Taking regular deep breaths may be helpful, as may massaging the abdomen.

This pain arises in the large intestine (colon), which starts low in the right side of the abdomen, rises to a point high under the liver, crosses the upper mid-section, and rises high under the diaphragm on the left side before descending into the lower left side where it joins the rectum. This large bowel has a very heavy and powerful muscular coat, which gives it the force to expel the stool. When stimulated, this musculature can contract so powerfully that its blood supply is temporarily interrupted, causing a steady, aching pain if it continues for more than a minute or two. This spasm may involve only one portion or segment of the bowel at a time.

The stimulus that provokes this spasm may be the presence of a considerable amount of stool in the middle and lower portions of the bowel, or an accumulation of gas and liquid feces in the right side because the lower bowel has not been emptied adequately. In some persons, however, nervous tension, such as may arise in a race, may stimulate the colon to spasm even when it is empty. These persons may experience this at times other than running, when they have not only pain but loose bowel movements. Such individuals are said to have a "spastic colon."

The best way to avoid stitch in the side is to try to establish a regularity of bowel movements, which will enable you to run with a colon that, if not empty, is at least not overfull. Since the presence of food in the upper intestinal tract also provides a natural stimulus to normal peristaltic action in the colon, this is a good reason to run no sooner than 3 hours after a meal. If you have a spastic colon, even if it is only one that acts up when you run, your physician can give you a prescription for a medication that will temporarily block the nerve impulses that produce spasm in the colon. This tablet can be taken from 1½ to 2 hours before you run.

You may have heard or read that stitch is caused by a spasm of the diaphragm. Most of you will have had hiccups —a spasm of the diaphragm—and will realize that the feeling and reaction are quite different. No one, to my knowledge, has yet demonstrated a sustained spasm of the diaphragm that can produce the type of pain encountered in a stitch, or produced it in the left side of the abdomen below the level of the umbilicus. Spasm of the colon has been recognized for a long time, is known to produce that type of pain, and the blanched appearance of the spastic bowel can be reproduced when the abdomen is opened for surgery by simply touching the colon or handling it gently.

Does the foregoing apply equally to men and women? Yes. If certain injuries are specific to one gender or the other, medical investigators haven't yet discovered them. It is true that female bone structure is on the average lighter than male, which, in theory, should predispose women and girls to more fractures. High school and college female runners, in fact, have a slightly higher rate of injury than their male counterparts. However, most researchers are inclined to ascribe this difference to acculturation: Female runners by and large were not as physically active in childhood and adolescence as boys. Hence, female bones were not accustomed to the stress of active running during the early formative years.

In addition, women have far less male hormone and thus cannot increase muscle size and mass to the extent that men can. But, again, no one has proved that this hormonal difference is a direct cause of injury in female runners.

Consequently, women should not read this book any "differently" from men, nor anticipate any specific gender-related injuries. The advice on running applies equally to both sexes.

Finally, a word about treatment: Some of the measures recommended for injuries must be performed by medical personnel—X rays, casting, and surgery, of course. On the other hand, many injuries are minor, and experienced runners often manage strains, pulls, and sprains themselves. This is not to denigrate the need for or usefulness of physicians (although it's true that many seasoned runners insist on being treated only by a physician who's also a runner). Rather it emphasizes the runner's knowledge of and confidence in his or her body. Among the many virtues of regular running is the intimate acquaintance that one develops with one's body. As you follow your running program, you will get to know your body—its structure, weak points, strong points, idiosyncrasies, its "Achilles heels"—better than you have ever known it and better than anyone else could know it.

Thus runners tend to look after their own aches and pains. They also develop the close relationship with the body which allows them to distingiush between recognizably minor problems and major damage—severe pain that doesn't diminish, inordinate swelling, excruciating tenderness to the touch. You will of necessity sharpen your own judgment on your body's responses to exercise and act accordingly. But, when in doubt seek help. That is still sound advice.

When You Can't Run

There may be times when you are physically unable to run, usually because of an injury that makes running difficult or impossible but doesn't incapacitate you otherwise. In the meantime, you don't want to lose the level of training and conditioning you have achieved. What do you do then?

Swimming is an excellent way to maintain your aerobic capacity without bearing weight on your legs. The only drawback is that you must be able to swim well enough to go the distance that will be equivalent to what you have been running. For example, swimming 200 yards at a steady pace is roughly equivalent to running 1 mile because of the increased resistance of the water.

If you can use your feet and legs to pedal a bicycle, but just cannot bear weight on them, riding a conventional bicycle or a stationary exercise bicycle is excellent aerobic exercise. Because you have to move the weight of the regular bicycle and thus encounter more air resistance, covering a mile by cycling uses about the same amount of energy as running that distance. If you can use only one leg effectively, you can still use the stationary bicycle. (This is a bit more difficult and dangerous with the conventional bicycle.)

You should be able to keep up with your flexibility and strength exercises, although they may have to be modified somewhat if you are unable to put weight on one or both feet. Deep-breathing exercises also may be useful if you can't swim or ride a bicycle. They help to keep the muscles of breathing in tone against the time you will return to aerobic exercise.

This is also a time to be especially careful about how much you eat and drink. Unless you are regularly cycling or swimming while your injury is healing, you probably won't be expending as many calories in energy costs. So you run the risk of gaining some unwanted fat weight. Strict moderation should be the dietary rule when you are unable to run.

STRETCHING EXERCISES

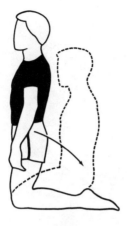

figure 1 Quadriceps stretching. Kneel down and then lower your trunk slowly until touching your feet with your buttocks. Hold for 10 seconds and return to your starting position. Repeat 4 times.

figure 2 Hamstring stretching. Sit on the floor with your legs spread apart at a 45-degree angle. Reach forward with both hands to grab your left leg below the knee, keeping the leg fully extended, and pull your body down toward it. Return to your starting position and repeat on the right side. Hold your position each time for 10 seconds. Repeat 4 times.

figures 3-a and **3-b** Low back stretching. In a seated position on the floor, draw your legs toward your trunk, crossing them in front of you. Reach forward, grabbing your left foot with your right hand and right foot with your left hand, and pull your trunk slowly down toward your knees. Hold for 10 seconds. Repeat 4 times.

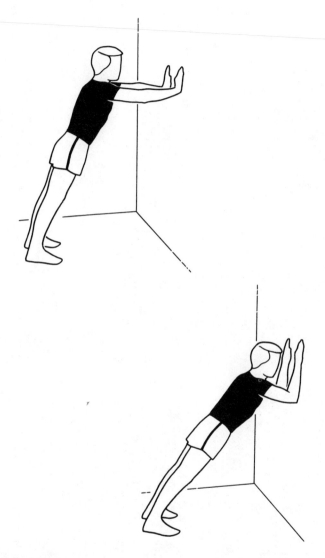

figures 4-a and **4-b** Calf stretching. Stand facing the wall with your feet 12 inches apart and about 3 feet away from the wall. Lean forward placing your palms flat against the wall. Bend your elbows until they touch the wall. Hold for 10 seconds and return to your starting position. Repeat 4 times.